And on the Eighth Day
God Created the Yankees

And on the Eighth Day God Created the

YANKEES

by

Vincent Bove, SDB

haven books
Division of Logos International
Plainfield, N.J. 07060

The author's share of the profits from the sale of this book are not for his personal use, but they are designated to be used for the Christian education of youth as conducted by the Salesians of St. John Bosco.

AND ON THE EIGHTH DAY GOD CREATED THE YANKEES
Published by Haven Books/Logos International in cooperation with Don Bosco Publications, New Rochelle, New York.
Copyright © 1981 by The Salesian Society, Inc.
All Rights Reserved
Printed in the United States of America
Library of Congress Catalog Card Number: 81-80696
International Standard Book Number: 0-88270-514-8
Logos International
Plainfield, New Jersey

To Thurman Lee Munson
(June 7, 1947-August 2, 1979)

"Our Captain and Leader has not left us—
    Today, tomorrow, this year, next . . .
Our endeavors will reflect our love and admiration for him."

(From monument dedicated in honor of Thurman Munson at Yankee Stadium.)

Contents

Thurman Munson

**Foreword by
Mrs. Thurman Munson**

Baseball players are more than individuals with athletic abilities. They are men with heart, mind, spirit, and soul. These men need to turn to someone who can fulfill these areas of their beings and that person is God. Sometimes I think children look up to ballplayers and make them bigger than life. I think it is so important for children to become aware of the things in life that are much more important than baseball. These things include looking up to God and having a real, deep faith in Him.

Baseball players certainly need to have this deeply personal faith in God. This is because there are often many tough times in the world of baseball. Once players begin to forget how they achieved their status, why they are there, or where their gift comes from, they are headed for trouble. I've seen this happen to some players and it is quite unfortunate. But the players who seem to be the happiest and who have the strength to get through the difficult times are most often the players who possess this deep faith in God. It is not something that has to be bragged about, but it is something that has to be lived.

Thurman was a player who really lived this life of faith in the baseball world. His faith naturally expressed itself in his actions. Thurman had a deep faith in God and this is something I think many people realized about him. He was a man who had his priorities in order. Thurman loved God, he loved his wife, and he loved his children. He made no bones about it, his family was extremely important to him. Thurman always put his wife and children far above his baseball stardom. People who knew Thurman saw the love he had for his family and they respected him for it. He was admired for this, more than I ever had realized during his lifetime.

After Thurman's death, thousands of letters have come to me. These letters are filled with great love for Thurman. He was a very reserved person before the press so the image created of him as being a coarse, gruff individual was an image far from the truth. People have written to me of the twinkle that they saw in his eye, the love that they realized was in his heart, the way he cried when he heard certain stories of handicapped children. They remember Thurman as a man who visited hospitals, who phoned the sick, and who did all these things without the media ever knowing about it.

Thurman had a very special love for young people. I did not know of the many things he did for young people until after his death. Then I began to receive countless letters that told me about the charities he was involved with for young people. Thurman did so much good, but never for publicity; he did it because he really had love in his heart.

Thurman was a spiritual man. He expressed this spirituality in many beautiful and spiritual poems he wrote. He was extremely grateful to God for his three children. He showed his gratitude to God for being blessed with a happy family by reaching out to others who were less fortunate than himself.

I think the dedication of this book in Thurman's honor is very appropriate. I know how much Thurman would have wanted to be a part of a book like this- -and now he is. This is such a thoughtful payment to him for the goodness that he represented to so many young pople.

Instead of thinking how terrible it is for me to have lost Thurman, I honestly feel very grateful to God for the time we shared together and for the wonderful memories I will always cherish. What I had was very beautiful; it is something I know many people never have. I had this great joy and I had it for a long time, so I am grateful.

I have three children in whom I see Thurman reflected each and every day. It is so fulfilling for me to think of all the blessings I have rather than to feel self-pity over what I have lost. The Lord has shown me that He is with me. He has given me the faith, courage, and strength to move on.

I believe that everything that has happened to me has not been without the presence of God. At first, Thurman's death was extremely difficult. But with time and faith I grew stronger. I still have difficult times but I know how to deal with them so much better. The Lord has carried me through my difficult times. I know He will continue to do so. He helped me so wonderfully during the ordeal surrounding Thurman's death. He continues to give me all the strength and courage I need. God alone has been the source of my strength and courage. Without His help I would have given up a long time ago.

Finally, I think the greatest message I could possibly share with you is that when things seem to be the toughest, realize that you are never alone. God is always with you. Also, remember that when things are going well for you, these things are coming from God.

Diana L. Munson

—Diana Munson

Introduction

The home of the New York Yankees since its opening on April 18, 1923, mammoth Yankee Stadium is considered by most sports authorities to be the most famous athletic arena in the United States. A good part of its fame can be traced to the Yankees' phenomenal baseball success and their many heroes who have played in it, including such greats as Babe Ruth, Lou Gehrig, Joe DiMaggio, and Mickey Mantle. The stadium has played host to thirty of their thirty-two World Series, with the Yankees winning all of their twenty-two World Championships, there.

(Prior to the building of Yankee Stadium, the Yankees played in the Polo Grounds from 1913-22 and, as the New York Highlanders, played at the Hilltop Park on 168th Street and Broadway.)

Yankee Stadium, located at 161st Street and

River Avenue in the Bronx, was designed by the Osborne Engineering Company of Cleveland, Ohio, and built by the White Construction Company of New York. Construction began on May 5, 1922, and it was completed the following April at a cost of $2,305,000.

The Stadium opened on April 18, 1923, with the Yankees defeating Boston 4-1. Babe Ruth hit the first stadium home run and the winning pitcher was Bob Shawkey, who threw out the first ball on Golden Anniversary Day in 1973.

Upon completion, the stadium was composed of massive three-deck concrete and steel stands and wooden bleachers. Later, the wooden bleachers were replaced by concrete stands. In 1923 the Yankees enlarged the left field stands (mezzanine and upper) and in 1937, the right field stands (lower, mezzanine and upper).

The playing field covers 3.5 acres, and the stadium plus surrounding grounds cover 11.6 acres.

Lights were installed in 1946 (2,400,000 watts) and a new scoreboard was installed in 1950. By 1959, the Yankees were ready to add a new board with the first changeable message area at a major league park in America. Now the new Yankee Stadium has the new scoreboard which is 560 feet long and twenty-four feet high, except for the dramatic "Telscreen" which reaches a height of forty feet at its center, and features "instant replay capabilities." The board is the most modern, up-to-date facility in any baseball stadium in the country. And while capturing the new, the board-like Yankee Stadium itself holds onto the proud Yankee history, with the famous stadium facade gracing the top of the board.

The first night game played at the stadium was on May 28, 1946, when the Yankees were defeated by the Washington Senators 2-1.

In 1953, Yankee Stadium and the grounds were sold to Earl and Arnold Johnson of Kansas City. Two years later, the Johnsons sold the stadium and grounds to John William Cox, a Chacago banker. The Yankee grounds were then sold to the Knights of Columbus. In 1962, Mr. Cox donated as a gift a "substantial amount" of stock in the corporation he headed (which owned Yankee Stadium) to Rice University in Houston, Texas.

In 1938, the Yankees and the Red Sox—*the* baseball rivalry—drew 81,841 fans for a Memorial Day doubleheader, a stadium record. Since that time the Yankees have cut down on the number of seats, and now have a capacity for 57,545.

In center field at Yankee Stadium—430 feet from home plate—are three monuments erected in memory of Babe Ruth, former manager Miller Huggins, and Lou Gehrig. Behind them are wall plaques honoring General Manager Edward G. Barrow, and Colonel Jacob Ruppert. To their left is a plaque commemorating the visit of Pope Paul VI in 1965, and there are also plaques honoring Joe DiMaggio and Mickey Mantle which the two greats presented to each other at Mickey Mantle's uniform retirement ceremony in 1969. There are also plaques honoring Casey Stengel and Joe McCarthy, and an additional plaque has been placed in center field in the memory of the great Yankee captain, Thurman Munson.

In addition to Mantle's retirement, other nostalgic events in stadium history include the tearful farewell appearances of a dying Lou Gehrig (July 4, 1939) and Babe Ruth (June 13, 1948). The annual Old-Timers Day, held each summer, has become a highlight for fans seeing old heroes one more time. Since 1965, the Yankees have given away thousands of baseball bats, caps, jackets, mugs, T-shirts, and photo albums in highly popular promotional dates for youngsters. Thousands of seats are additionally provided for underprivileged children.

During the winter of 1966-67, Yankee Stadium was given a new look as ninety tons of paint turned the stadium white on the outside and royal blue on the inside. All of the bleacher seats were converted to fiberglass at that time. Inside, fans were treated to a "Telephonic Hall of Fame," which allowed them to hear the recorded voices of great names from the past and receive playing tips from the current players. The modernization and refurbishing program gave the stadium its most complete face-lifting since 1923.

In 1972, Mayor John V. Lindsay for the city and the Yankees, agreed on a plan whereby the stadium would be completely renovated during

1974-75, while the Yankees shared Shea Stadium with the New York Mets. The Yankees would then return to the fully remodeled Yankee Stadium in time for the 1976 baseball season. After the City of New York took over the ownership of the structure in 1972, the Yankees signed a thirty-year lease to remain in Yankee Stadium. In 1973, a group headed by George M. Steinbrenner III purchased the club and quickly restored the pride and glory of the men in pinstripes.

The fully remodeled Yankee Stadium re-opened on April 15, 1976, with the Yankees beating Minnesota 11-4. Rudy May started the game, while reliever Dick Tidrow picked up the win. The Minnesota Twins' Dan Ford hit the first home run in the new park and, two days later, Thurman Munson hit the Yankees' first home run.

The Yankees apparently found the "new" home to their liking as they responded with the American League pennant in 1976 and in 1977—their first World Series in 15 years. Reggie Jackson set a record by hitting three home runs in one game at the stadium as the Yankees defeated the Los Angeles Dodgers, four games to two.

The Yankees successfully defended the World Championship in 1978 by defeating the Dodgers for the second straight year. This capped a season that found the New Yorkers fourteen games behind in July and clinching the American League East pennant in a one-game play-off against Boston in October.

The 1979 season was a disappointment to the Yankees, who found themselves in a fourth place finish. But the Yankee fans demonstrated their continuous support as over two-and-half million people visited the stadium—the highest attendance mark in the American League.

In 1980 the New York Yankees recaptured the Eastern Division Championship of The American League. Along with this, the team broke American League records for home and away attendance.

With this tremendous baseball heritage, fans all over the world can surely agree that *And on the Eighth Day God Created the Yankees.*

And on the Eighth Day
God Created the Yankees

Yogi Berra

Dear Fans,

I have been involved in major league baseball since 1947. I am grateful for the gift of my career which the Lord Jesus has given me.

My experiences in baseball have given me many different insights about life. In particular, I would like all of you to remember the basics — especially in reference to respecting God's commandments.

Always strive to do your best on and off any field. Be a good sport during times of victory or defeat and be assured that you and your loved ones will receive blessings in return.

Yogi Berra

Yogi Berra

A few years ago, I can remember hearing a remark about Yogi Berra from a fan at Yankee Stadium, "One hasn't really experienced the thrill of being in Yankee Stadium until he sees Yogi Berra."

Yogi Berra is certainly characteristic of the excitement of Yankee baseball. Yet, this is very ironic, for Yogi is a very simple and reserved man. He is a man who is very sensitive to the needs of others. For instance, Yogi finds it very difficult to visit children who are confined to hospitals. Yet, Yogi realizes his responsibility as a Christian, and so he visits children often.

Yogi remembers a particular incident when he visited a young boy in a hospital. The doctors had given very little hope that this boy would live. Yogi was deeply saddened by the boy's condition. But, in spite of the doctors' prognosis, God had other plans for this young boy. What great joy Yogi had when he met this young boy enjoying a game at Yankee Stadium a few months later. The youth had completely recovered.

Yogi has also participated in the Catholic Youth Organization, and he has spoken to youth groups and individuals at various functions throughout his career.

Yogi Berra slamming his 250th career home run. (*N.Y. Daily News* photo.)

Johnny Blanchard

Dear Fans,

I am a recovering alcoholic and have not taken the chemical for five years. Believe me, I wish I had not been drinking during my sports career. My days in baseball would have lasted for several more years. But I thought it was macho or big time to drink and "be one of the boys." How wrong I was! My life was really miserable for many years. Then my higher power—Almighty God—somehow turned me around to seek help for this illness.

My advice to you is: *if you are not taking any drugs now, don't start.* It will do you no good, but it could lead you to suicide, loneliness, or trouble with the police. In general, it will simply mess up your life. To those of you who are on the stuff, I want you to look at yourself. Ask yourself, "What does this stuff do for me? What harm has it caused me? How many friends have I lost? Do I argue and fight with my parents?

Do I have bad companions? Do I attend church, or have I just fallen away from God?" When you get high, the last place where you would like to be is church. Now, really, are you a leader or a follower?

Just remember that you cannot have any self-respect while you are on drugs. You may think you are cool but, in reality, you become nothing short of a useless human being. But I am living proof that this can all change. Ask for help and someone out there will help you.

Let me put it this way—sit down with a pencil and paper and make two columns. In the first column write down all the good things that come from using drugs. In the other column write down all the bad things. Then number them. If the good things outnumber the bad, then go ahead and use drugs. But if the bad things outnumber the good, then do something about it.

Johnny Blanchard

God bless all of you,
Johnny Blanchard

Johnny Blanchard

Johnny Blanchard came to the New York Yankees primarily as a backup catcher and outfielder in 1959. He was to have six full years with the Yankees; he recalls those years as being the happiest of his life.

Johnny was a fine ballplayer for the Yankees. This was realized but often hidden behind the exceptional Yankee catchers Yogi Berra and Elston Howard. Yet, Johnny humbly accepted his backup role during his Yankee years. He was proud to be part of the team as a second-string, and sometimes even a third-string, player. But credit is certainly due to Johnny Blanchard. When duty called, he filled in for his Yankee teammates with fine defensive and offensive abilities. He could have been a star first-string player with a host of other major league teams.

Johnny Blanchard was a dedicated Yankee. When he heard of his being traded in 1963, he broke down and cried at the thought of having to finally give up his Yankee pin stripes. Yet, Johnny's joyful Yankee days come alive again each year when he returns to Yankee Stadium for the annual Old Timers Day game.

Johnny's message to youth is certainly one of profound sincerity and humility. It is his deepest desire for others to learn of the problems that the improper use of alcohol can create in any person's life.

Bobby Brown

Dear Fans,

I am a professional baseball player only because God has blessed me. Yet, I realize that He also gave me determination and effort so I could develop His gifts.

Continually strive to develop your own particular gifts. When you achieve success, learn to be at peace with yourself. But if you feel motivated to climb even greater heights, you must strive even harder.

Success comes when one is faithful in carrying out everyday responsibilities. So when you are carrying out a little obligation—no matter how small it seems—give it your best, for you will never do great things well unless you are faithful in small things.

Bobby Brown

Bobby Brown

Bobby Brown is a very young ballplayer with tremendous baseball talent. His speed makes him a dangerous base runner and a consistent defensive outfielder. Along with speed, "Uptown Bobby Brown" has exceptional power as a hitter.

I remember first meeting Bobby Brown about two years ago and hearing him ask with optimistic eagerness, "I wonder when I'll get a chance to play?" My answer to him was, "Your day will come, Bobby—patience." Bobby recently told me how much encouragement these words gave him, for he really believed his day to play would come.

It seems that Bobby's day has come. During the 1980 baseball season, Bobby participated in more major league games than ever before in his career. Bobby became a starting center fielder in August, following the unfortunate injury of his teammate Ruppert Jones. It is only a beginning, but it seems that Bobby Brown's day in professional baseball has certainly begun.

Bobby Brown enthusiastically says, "Young people are my greatest thrill." He spends many hours with young people at home in Eastville, Virginia. He enjoys meeting them right where they "hang out" rather than making formal appearances.

Rick Cerone

Dear Fans,

I would like to share with you my gratitude for a fine education. My education in grammar school, high school, and college has been Catholic throughout.

I grew up in Newark, New Jersey. At that time it was a very difficult place to grow up in and so it remains. I know that many of my friends who did not have the education I was privileged to receive, lost out. Without the positive influences which I know I had, these friends were more susceptible to the city's dangers. They fell prey to these dangers and unfortunately many of them are still affected by negative influences. I am so grateful for the many priests, brothers, and nuns who helped me avoid getting lost. They helped me keep a proper perspective on life. I owe my spiritual, mental, and physical upbringing to them and to the solid education which they helped me receive.

There has been one tremendous highlight in my life as a Catholic ballplayer. In 1973, I was eighteen years old and playing for the United States College All-Star Team. The team was involved in a world tournament and we were playing in Rome. I will never forget visiting the Holy Father who at that time was Pope Paul VI. Listening to the Pope speak in person left an unforgettable impression upon me. Here I was in Rome, visiting the Vatican, St. Peters, the Coliseum, and to highlight everything, I was able to meet the Pope. It is a memory I will always cherish deeply.

Keep the Faith, #10
Rick Cerone

Rick Cerone

Incredible pressure was placed upon Rick Cerone as New York fans anxiously waited to see if Thurman Munson's shoes would be filled. Also, would the greatest catching tradition in baseball, as represented by Dickey, Berra, Howard, and Munson, be continued?

Rick courageously accepted this awesome challenge. His reputation as a fine defensive catcher and respectable clutch hitter was obviously deserved, as he quickly proved himself in his Yankee pin stripes.

Rick's appreciation and love for the Yankee

uniform had been sparked by his own love for "America's Baseball Team" as a Newark, New Jersey, youth. Rick's efforts on the field will definitely continue to be inspired by his appreciation for being able to wear the Yankee uniform and his love for his countless back yard fans.

Rick Cerone enjoys making private and personal appearances to youth in hospitals. He also enjoys giving talks to various groups of young people.

In 1980, Rick was the National Chairman of the Leukemia Foundation. He has also done work with handicapped young people through the Special Olympics Program. Through these efforts Rick has been a source of inspiration and encouragement to many young people.

In July of 1980, the Kidney Foundation made a pregame presentation at Yankee Stadium to Rick Cerone. He was honored for his efforts on behalf of New York's Third International Transplant Olympics.

During a conversation between Rick and myself in the Yankee clubhouse, he showed me a recent award, the "Northward Educational and Cultural Center Award." This award was presented to Rick on September 18, 1980, for his "outstanding athletic ability and gentlemanly characteristics which set a standard for Newark's Northward youngsters." Rick was especially pleased with this award since he had been a youngster who "grew up in the streets" of Newark.

Bucky Dent

Dear Fans,

I was very fortunate to have been given a very good Christian foundation as a boy. My home always had a strong Christian atmosphere.

Later on, my Christian life continued to develop. I had very profound Christian experiences in athletics during my high school days. In particular, I was involved with a fellowship of Christian athletes—my high school football teammates. We were proud of the motto of our helmets which read, "Faith and Pride." Our team certainly had an unbelievable faith in God and a healthy pride in using the gifts He had given us. Never will I forget the deep Christian experiences of those days.

Besides football, baseball was also a very important part of my life during my earlier days. As a young man I began to dream of a future in professional baseball. The Lord has certainly blessed me by allowing me to fulfill that dream.

You must also have a dream about your future. Remember that if you allow God to be a partner in your life, He will help you with all your dreams. But remember, the Lord expects your cooperation. You must be willing to give of yourself totally, that is, spiritually, mentally, emotionally, and physically.

Remember also that you will have failures during your efforts of fulfilling your dreams. But have faith in God always. God allows us to fail so that we may depend on Him more than ourselves and therefore truly grow as persons. When troubles come your way, it is so easy to quit, but these are times to believe totally in God, for He will give you strength to overcome all obstacles.

You will always have opportunities to achieve success and opportunities to take the easy way out. Have courage and put your faith in Christ, for He will help you fulfill your dreams.

Bucky Dent

Bucky Dent

Bucky Dent's highlights in the world of baseball are many. Ever since his major league career began with the Chicago White Sox in 1973, Bucky has played in three Championship Series, and a pair of World Series, and All-Star games.

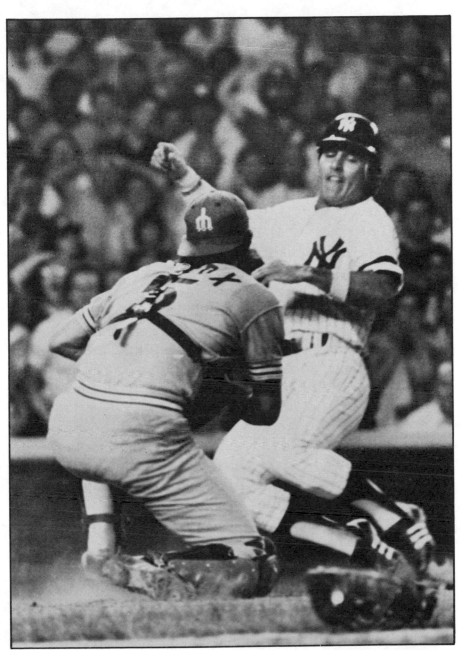

(Photo by Louis Requena.)

His homerun against the Boston Red Sox in 1978 propelled the Yankees into the play-offs. After helping the Yanks win these play-off games, he captured the distinctive World Series Most Valuable Player Award for his brilliant fielding and a .417 batting average in the famous 1978 classic. Bucky's exceptional fielding also enabled him to lead all American League shortstops throughout the 1980 season, and this sent him straight to the All-Star team.

Throughout the New York area, Bucky Dent is a household name. His popularity among youth is obvious as one sees "Bucky" stickers on the fenders of cars all over. Countless youths scream the name of "Bucky" in and outside of Yankee Stadium. Many of these same youths chose him as the Catholic Youth Organization's Most Popular Yankee of the 1978 season. Bucky proudly displays this trophy at his home.

Bucky is extremely aware of his blessings from God and of his responsibility for helping others by Christian service and example. He is especially attracted to helping handicapped youths. Bucky humbly believes that his work for these young people brings more inspiration to his own life than he can ever bring to theirs.

On August 4, 1980, Bucky was presented with a very special award before the game at Yankee Stadium. He had helped raise over $100,000 for handicapped children as the Honorary Chairman of the Easter Seals Softball Marathon. Bucky was deeply grateful for the recognition of his sincere commitment to helping America's handicapped, but he was more grateful to those same youths who have so greatly inspired him.

Brian Doyle

Dear Fans,

When I play baseball, it is not for the fans, nor for myself, but it is for Jesus Christ, my Lord! I believe baseball is my call to tell the world that Jesus is Lord!

I often speak to youngsters at clinics and even at my own baseball camp. Because of my experiences with the Yankees I am given tremendous respect. But, let us go one step further. I ask you to respect and understand the fact that I have also experienced Christ in my life, and I wish to share Him with you.

During my early years I was Christian only one hour per week at Sunday services. But, five years ago, my wife gave birth to a son, and this inspired me to reflect over my Christian background. I remembered the Old Testament story of Abraham and Issac. Then I realized how this story foretold the New Testament story of God offering up His only Son. Like never before, I became aware of what great love God had for me. God loved me so much that He gave up His only Son. And here was I with my newborn son. Would I be able to give him totally to God as He gave His Son for me? It was at this moment of profound reflection that my Christian walk began.

I know that God loves me and watches over me. Whether I have a great game or I bat 0 for 4 in a crucial game, I know God is there. I believe in the power of His love, a love which proved itself in the offering of His Son.

Scripture gives me the strength to realize that my faith in God has given me eternal life.

John 5:24

Brian Doyle

Brian Doyle

Anyone who appreciates baseball knows the tremendous value of a reliable backup ballplayer. Brian Doyle's contributions to the Yankee organization have been immeasurable.

Yankee fans will never forget Brian's most cherished Yankee experience. When Brian substituted for his injured teammate Willie Randolph in the 1978 World Series Classic, he hit an amazing .438 while playing fantastic defensive baseball.

Brian realizes that his baseball career is merely

a means of witnessing to a much greater value, a value that does not measure a man's success by his batting average but by his love.

Brian greatly enjoys giving talks and testimonies of his Christian faith to young people of all ages and denominations. He looks forward to the day when he can give even more energy to teaching the Word of God.

During the off-season Brian works at his own Christian baseball camp in Florida, which is dedicated to the total development of the athlete. Brian believes that the athlete can only truly be his best if he strives to develop spiritually, emotionally, physically, and mentally.

Many are drawn to Brian's constant, good Christian example. One cannot fail to be impressed by Willie Randolph's sincere admiration for Brian as the letter which Willie wrote shows. I also distinctly remember a time of Christian sharing which Brian Doyle, Reggie Jackson, and I had together one evening in the Yankee clubhouse. Afterwards, Reggie Jackson told me, "Now Brian Doyle is a man whom I call a Christian. I am constantly drawing good example and encouragement from him. Whenever I need a little boost, I go and share a few moments with Brian Doyle and I thank God for him."

Before the 1981 season began, Brian was traded by the Yankees. His teammates will miss him but the Lord will be willing to use Brian Doyle wherever he is.

Mike Ferraro

Dear Fans,

Do things because of a deep desire to excel rather than because you feel forced to. Don't let things which you have to work at become a burden. If it's something that you know will help you, cultivate a desire to excel.

Our Lord puts you on earth with certain gifts. You must make sure you use them properly. Your desire to use your gifts must be expressed through hard work and practice.

Working as a coach with the Yankees, I realize that the players who want to become better base runners, hitters, fielders, bunters, etc., do become better when they place a loving desire in their work rather than treating training as a burden. So put that desire into everything

you do, whether it be at school, work, or play—
and you will excel.

Mike Ferraro

Mike Ferraro

Yankee Coach Mike Ferraro

Before becoming the Yankee third-base coach in 1979, Mike Ferraro had played for four years in the majors and coached for five years in the Yankee farm system.

As a major league ballplayer, Mike tied a defensive record by making eleven assists at third base in a nine-inning game on September 14, 1968.

His minor league management posted a 331-221 won-loss record which included three championship teams.

Mike has two children. He also has a sincere concern for other children, which encouraged him to be the Director of Recreation for Youth in Kingston, New York, during the early seventies. In this position he was responsible for the formation of recreational programs for the underprivileged youth of the Kingston area.

Mike has sinced moved from Kingston but continues to realize the importance of properly guiding youth in the Christian manner. He continues to welcome invitations to help youth in whatever way he can.

Yankee coach Mike Ferraro accepts applause from fans prior to 1980 play-off game. (United Press International photo.)

Ed Figueroa

Dear Fans,

Remember to direct your energies toward your education ahead of participation in sports. You will not always be able to depend on atheletic abilities, but your education will be useful to you throughout your entire life. Make your education the first priority!

In regard to your parents, always listen to them, respect them, and be open to learning from them.

Watch your companions and select your friends very carefully. As a professional ballplayer I have many acquaintances. But a true friendship is a much deeper relationship. Therefore, a few good friends are of greater value than many acquaintances. Make sure that your companions are carefully chosen so that their influence on you may be positive.

Ed Figueroa (signature)

Ed Figueroa

Ed Figueroa

Shortly after Ed Figueroa expressed his views in his letter to youth, his Yankee career came to an end. As one reflects on Ed's letter, one realizes that Ed was sharing his present personal experience. In 1979, elbow problems hampered Ed's illustrious Yankee career, and Ed found it understandably difficult to regain his quality pitching status as a Yankee.

Yet, when Ed remembers his Yankee experiences, he will certainly have many favorable ones. Appreciated by "the Big Apple" fans and affectionately known as "Figgy," Ed won fifty-five games for "the Bronx Bombers" from 1976-78, including a twenty-game winning season. The victorious twenty-game winning season made Ed the only Puerto Rican in baseball history to accomplish such a feat. Also, Ed helped lead the Yanks to three World Series, which always appreciative Yankee fans will not easily forget.

Rich Gossage

Dear Fans,

I was never a good student, so I am extremely appreciative of my atheletic abilities. Sports have helped me set a wholesome pattern of living for myself. While many of my peers were hanging out and wasting time I was applying myself to improving my athletic talents. As a result of my participation in sports, the qualities of discipline, loyalty, and teamwork have become important aspects of my life.

Sports can teach these same values to everyone. I am glad that boys and girls have the opportunity to become more involved in sports. I failed my first year in school, so my younger sister caught up with me. Growing up side by side with her made me realize that athletic opportunities for girls were so very limited. But now girls can play on many different athletic teams and thereby enjoy a more active sports life. Therefore, the deeper values offered by sports can now be experienced firsthand by both girls and boys.

Make use of all the opportunities you have to receive a solid education. I had been in a fine parochial school until my parents could no longer afford it. But now my career makes a fine education possible for my children—an education which will help them grow totally in mind, body, and spirit. I am happy that I will be able to help them learn about their religion and their God.

Rich Gossage

Rich Gossage

Rich Gossage's first season as a Yankee—in 1978—earned him the Rolaids Relief Man of the Year Award and the *Sporting News* Fireman of the Year Award. His powerful right arm gave Rich the American League pitching lead of twenty-seven saves, along with dynamic appearances in the 1978 season's play-off, pennant, and World Series victories. He had another outstanding year in 1980.

"The Golden Goose" has a deep appreciation for the values which sports can offer to all. Rich began to learn these values in his very early school days and continues to learn them even as a Yankee superstar.

Rich enjoys the presence of youth. He especially realizes the importance of visiting the young who are confined to hospitals, and he does so whenever he can.

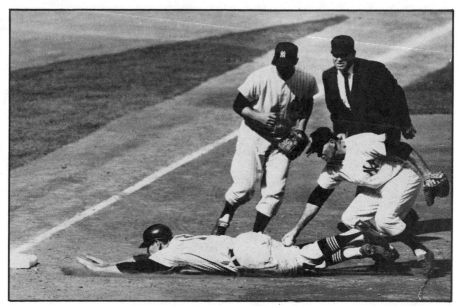

Bobby Richardson tagging Johnny Romano out at third. (Photo by *The New York Times.*)

Bobby Murcer loses his helmet as Kansas City Royals pitcher Lance Clemons stabs him with the ball during the fourth inning—Yanks vs. Kansas City, August 18, 1971. (*N.Y. Daily News* photo.)

Reggie Jackson hits 400th career homer on August 11, 1980. (Photo by Louis Requena.)

Yankee coach Mike Ferraro greets Reggie Jackson after his 400th homer. (Photo by Louis Requena.)

Ron Guidry on his way to a three-hit shutout. (*N.Y. Daily News* photo.)

Yankee catcher Dennis Werth and pitcher Ed Figueroa. (Photo by Louis Requena.)

Bucky Dent slides safely to home plate for his first and only inside-the-park home run of his career—May 15, 1980. (*N.Y. Daily News* photo.)

Bucky Dent receives an award for his service as Easter Seals Softball Marathon Chairman at Yankee Stadium—August 4, 1980.

Catcher Rick Cerone puts all his energy into a play. (Photo by Louis Requena.)

Bobby Brown greeted by Jim Spencer after a home run. (Photo by Louis Requena.)

Watchful Yogi Berra keeps alert during his days as Yankee manager. (Photo courtesy of New York Yankees.)

1980 NEW YORK YANKEES

First Row, Seated—BUCKY DENT, JIM HEGAN, YOGI BERRA, DICK HOWSER, CHARLEY LAU, MIKE FERRARO, STAN WILLIAMS, JEFF TORBORG.
Second Row, Seated—BOBBY MURCER, TOM UNDERWOOD, ERIC SODERHOLM, JOHNNY OATES, RUPPERT JONES, DENNIS WERTH, BOB WATSON, RICK CERONE.
Third Row—TEAM DOCTOR JOHN BONAMO, TRAINER GENE MONAHAN, OSCAR GAMBLE, BATTING PRACTICE PITCHER MICKEY SCOTT, BOBBY BROWN,
LUIS TIANT, JIM SPENCER, FRED STANLEY, LOU PINIELLA, REGGIE JACKSON, TRAINER BARRY WEINBERG, BATTING PRACTICE PITCHER DOUG MELVIN.
EQUIPMENT MANAGER PETE SHEEHY.
Back Row—WILLIE RANDOLPH, BULLPEN CATCHER DOM SCALA, TIM LOLLAR, TOMMY JOHN, RON GUIDRY, RICH GOSSAGE, RON DAVIS, DOUG BIRD, RUDY MAY.
Seated on Ground—BATBOYS: PATRICK CASSIDY, ERROL TOULON, JR., STEVEN D'ANGELO.

68

Memorial for the late and great Thurman Munson—August 6, 1979, at Yankee Stadium. (Photo by Louis Requena.)

The New York Yankees dugout. (Photo by Louis Requena.)

The Yankees, led by manager Dick Howser, center in jacket, thank the fans for their year-long support after clinching the 1980 Eastern Division title—October 6, 1980. (*N.Y. Daily News* photo.)

Munson in 1978, the summer prior to his tragic death, warming up at Yankee Stadium. (Photo by Brother Vince Bove.)

Ron Guidry with Special Olympian John Hughes. (Photo courtesy of Special Olympics.)

Ron Guidry and Reggie Jackson give their love and support to participants in the Special Olympics. (Photo courtesy of Special Olympics.)

The late and beloved coach Elston Howard observes his players in action.

Yankee Stadium—after its renovations.

Ron Guidry

Dear Fans,

From the earliest days of my youth, my upbringing was strictly Catholic. Then and now, I have pride in saying that I love my Catholic religion.

I pray often and I know God hears all my prayers. He may not answer them in the way I desire, but He knows what is best for me.

My goal has always been to be a professional baseball player. Yet, I know that being a successful major league pitcher is a gift from Christ and no one else.

I say a prayer before each game that I pitch. It is not a prayer for victory, it is a prayer of gratitude for my health and a plea for God's continued blessings.

There are so many more important things in life than winning baseball games. When I win a game I know it is God's grace. When I lose, I know there are many people with more serious problems.

All of us have crossroads in life. But when they come our way, we must place our faith in God and realize He will inspire us to make the right decisions. Our hope must be in God!

Let us always strive to make our decisions with the inspiration and wisdom of Christ. He alone can truly inspire us and help us to inspire others.

Ron Guidry

Ron Guidry

Impressive! Ron Guidry personifies the preceding word in many different ways. "Louisiana Lightning's" Yankee achievements are extremely impressive. In 1977, Ron posted a 16-7 record with a 2.82 ERA. In 1978, Ron's victory record soared to a fantastic twenty-five wins while having only three losses. Baseball's coveted Cy Young Award followed this achievement along with *Sporting News* Athlete of the Year and Man of the Year Awards. In 1979, Ron led the American League with a fine 2.78 ERA while posting an 18-8 year. Of course Ron's specialty is his awesome fast ball and tremendous slider,

which has earned him over 800 strikeouts as a Yankee.

Far beyond what his baseball statistics echo is Ron Guidry's impressive personality. He is a man who knows exactly what his most important priorities are. Ron is totally aware of where his athletic abilities come from and who he must be grateful to.

Ron's special Christian service to youth comes through his efforts toward the Special Olympics Program. This program is the world's largest program of sports training and athletic competition for youth who are mentally handicapped. Ron's inspiration to be of service to this very noble program comes from his younger brother, Travis, who is one of America's many mentally handicapped youth. Ron has a very special devotion to Travis, one which certainly inspires Ron to reach out to youth who share his brother's cross.

On July 22, 1979, Ron received a most coveted award for being the pride of the Special Olympics Program. Eunice Kennedy Shriver, the founder and president of this international program, bestowed the Spirit of the Special Olympics Award upon Ron before thousands of fans at Yankee Stadium. While doing so she told him, "Because you have shared your life with your very special brother . . . because whenever you have free time you have visited Special Olympians . . . because of the marvelous example you have set for the youth of America in unselfishness and self-sacrifice."

Dick Howser

Dear Fans,

I firmly believe that all people, whether they be athletes or not, need a spiritual dimension in their lives.

My Methodist religion has always been a great source of strength for me, and I am grateful to my parents for their Christian example which has always encouraged the spiritual element in my own life.

Faith is a must for everyone, for it brings proper direction and character to the lives of those who follow its ways.

All of us must learn how to turn to God often, not only during crisis situations but also when things are going well. Interestingly, I have come to realize that most good ballplayers have a tremendous religious attitude which helps them to live balanced lives. Ballplayers with this source of strength survive even the most difficult times, while many people without a religious dimension often cannot survive even the best of times. Without religious ideals there is a lack of balance.

Make sure that you develop your own religious beliefs so that you may have proper direction and a balanced character in your own life. Remember that cheating, deception, and any other vices never bring true happiness or success. Only with God can you ever become a person who is properly directed, a person who has tremendous character.

Dick Howser

Dick Howser

In 1980, Yankee Manager Dick Howser made baseball history while managing his team all the way to the American League's Eastern Division Championship. He was only the fourth manager in major league history to win as many as 100 games as a rookie.

Dick was a major leaguer for eight years before becoming a Yankee coach in 1969. He remained a dependable coach for ten years before accepting his managerial position with the Yanks in 1979.

Dick Howser deeply believes that youths need spiritual direction in their lives. His favorite way of impressing this value to them is by good example and by giving talks to various gatherings of young people.

Reggie Jackson

Dear Fans,

Remember that athletes are only human beings, full of imperfections like yourselves. You must always have a realistic attitude toward them, an attitude which is grounded in respect rather than worship.

I believe it is very important to show respect toward individuals who live up to their obligations and responsibilities whether or not you like the individuals involved. This is because respect is a virtue which goes far beyond the emotion of liking. Always respect but never worship anyone because worship is an exaggeration.

Many athletes have an exaggerated public image. This is unfair to the athlete, since he is only a human being. The only one who ever walked this earth who deserves such praise is Jesus Christ. He alone deserves to be worshiped and emulated. We can certainly put great expectations upon Christ but not upon athletes, for their images are often shattered because of human imperfections. The perfect image of Christ can never be shattered because He is God.

God has given unique gifts to each and every one of us. Remember that you must be truthful to God and to yourselves regarding these gifts. Each person has a very serious obligation and responsibility to develop his own particular gifts. Do not shortchange God, yourselves, or the many people you can help by failing to develop your gifts.

Remember also to pray, but try not to be concerned about asking for things. God will give you what you need if you remember to praise Him and to be grateful to Him for His countless blessings. Gratitude to God is so very important! It is so easy to complain when things go wrong, but how often do you thank God when so many things are going well?

Finally, I would like to share this favorite prayer of mine: "Lord, guide me, lead me, direct me. Do with my life as you see fit." May all of you grow in your relationship with God, for He alone deserves our worship and praise.

Reggie Jackson

Reggie Jackson enjoys the sailing of his 400th home run over the right field fence at Yankee Stadium. (*N.Y. Daily News* photo.)

Reggie Jackson

Reggie Jackson is perhaps the most well-known active player in the major leagues today. He has played major league baseball since 1967. In this thirteen-year span, he has played on eight championship series teams, five world series teams, and ten all-star teams. He stands not only as a national sports hero, but an international sports figure as well.

Besides his impressive baseball achievements, Reggie's humanitarian services are also very respectable. He is constantly offering his time and services to youth. He does so by often visiting youths who are sick and by donating to many different charities.

Watching Reggie over the course of the 1980 season authenticated these words which he once shared with me, "I don't like to sign autographs. I don't think they are real. But if I ever see a crippled child, I will always stop, since an autograph for them has an entirely different meaning."

I have often seen Reggie turn down giving autographs. Yet, I have often been inspired as I watched him go out of his way to give of himself graciously to individuals who were handicapped.

Tommy John

Dear Fans,

Being a baseball player demands a tremendous amount of work, dedication, discipline, and, of course, talent. Each and every one of us has a unique, God-given talent. That is God's gift to us. Our gift to Him is to develop that talent to its fullest. We can't all be pro athletes, but we can strive for the best in whatever we do.

The area that demands the most from us is discipline. This discipline has three forms: physical, mental and spiritual. Physical discipline requires us to develop our bodies to the fullest extent without abusing them with drugs, drinking, or any other body-destroying agents. We should eat properly to give our bodies a chance to use the talents God has given to us.

Mental discipline is the second aspect which demands our attention. To be mentally tough, we should study hard, try to retain what we have studied, and do our best in school. We owe this effort in schoolwork to the ones we love—our parents, our pastors, our priests, and our God.

The third and last area of discipline is spiritual. We need this discipline when we are in church. If our minds are distracted while we are listening to God's Word, we must learn to be tough. The Bible is our rule book of life, and it helps us live full lives as God would have us. Yet, to do so we must obey the rules. We have to be spiritually disciplined.

These three disciplines will not assure us of eternal life. We must go one step further and accept Jesus Christ as our Savior. But these three disciplines will give us a better life on earth and the chance to take that extra step. Let us take the step, accept Jesus, and prepare to experience eternal life with God.

In Christ's Love,
Tommy John
Philippians 4:13

Tommy John

In 1975, Dr. Frank Jobe performed a serious and delicate operation on Tommy John's left elbow. Afterwards, Tommy John was told that his baseball career had come to an end.

But Tommy John's courage and faith brought him once again to spectacular baseball per-

formances. As a Los Angeles Dodger pitcher in 1976, Tommy received the National League Comeback Player of the Year award. In 1977, he won an amazing twenty games, and in 1978, he totaled twenty-one victories.

Tommy, affectionately referred to by his fans as TJ, attributes his success to more than a natural talent. TJ is a man of physical, mental and, most importantly, spiritual discipline. It is no wonder that this well-rounded man of God has been abundantly blessed.

Tommy has a tremendous concern for young people which shows itself in many different ways:

1) Honorary Chairman of the Multiple Sclerosis Read-a-Thon in Bergen County, New Jersey.

2) Honorary Chairman of the Boy Scouts Hole-in-One Fund in Bergen County, New Jersey.

3) Sports Chairman of the Cystic Fibrosis Society in Orange County, California.

4) Sports Chairman of the Ronald McDonald Houses in Los Angeles and Orange County, California.

5) Golf Tourney Host (four consecutive years) for cancer research and treatment at the Children's Hospital in Los Angeles, California.

6) Active member of the Fellowship of Christian Athletes in New Jersey and California.

Tommy John certainly has a God-given talent when it comes to playing baseball. Yet, he keeps this gift in its proper perspective by being aware of its source and by showing appreciation for it through his Christian service.

Ruppert Jones

Dear Fans,

As a professional athlete I realize that many people look up to me. I felt the same way toward stars when I was young. But all people are important, since each has his own God-given talents which must be developed. So work on developing your talents. But remember, no one is perfect. Therefore, be understanding when failures come to you and to others.

God has blessed me with a professional baseball career. But I made a mistake with sports. During my school days I exaggerated the importance of sports and avoided my books. Learn from my mistake and avoid minimizing your talents by setting only one goal. Be the well-rounded person the Lord meant you to be. Develop all of your talents rather then placing too much emphasis on only a few of them.

You must also have the proper attitude toward suffering. In the last three years I have undergone three operations. At first, each one brought me great disappointment. But later, each proved to be a real character builder. My physical trials have made me more aware of who I am and of where I am going.

Finally, many of you are familiar with the movie "Star Wars." In it, as in life, two powerful forces exist. Darth Vader represents the evil force. In direct contrast, Luke Skywalker represents goodness. As individuals, we can identify with and actually live out roles that correspond with either of these two forces. We can cultivate a dark, devilish force or a bright, angelic one. Let each of us seek to cultivate the force within us that is angelic!

Ruppert Jones

Ruppert Jones

Ruppert Jones

The enormous center field in Yankee Stadium has a player with the swiftness and ability of a cheetah as he fields baseballs. Ruppert Jones plays his center field turf with classy distinction. In his short period with the Yanks he has already thrilled the Big Apple's fans with his fine speed and remarkably accurate throwing arm.

Ruppert's defensive abilities are paralleled by his offensive talents. At the young age of

twenty-five, he already has had over sixty major league home runs, eighty stolen bases, and over 500 base hits. The Bronx Bombers have certainly acquired a very versatile new addition who has World Champion caliber.

Ruppert holds his outstanding baseball talent in its proper perspective. He realizes that being a well-rounded person means that one should concentrate on developing all of one's talents. Also, Ruppert knows by practical experience that one should always be open to the positive characteristics that difficulties can bring to an individual's life.

Ruppert had ample time for reflection regarding the trials he writes about in his letter. On August 25, 1980, Ruppert Jones crashed into a center field wall while chasing a fly ball in the Oakland A's stadium. The result of this accident was a severe concussion and a separated right shoulder, which forced Ruppert to miss the remainder of the 1980 Yankee campaign. The injuries had totally knocked Ruppert unconscious. Bobby Murcer and Bob Watson had both spoken to me afterwards about this incident, and both had believed at the time that Ruppert had been killed.

During his recovery, Ruppert had told me he was glad to be alive and that he realized, "The man upstairs really cared about me."

Sufferings and difficulties certainly bring an important insight into the meaning of life for both young and old. How important it is to appreciate the Christian value of suffering, which offers opportunity to grow deeper in the faith of Jesus.

Rudy May

Dear Fans,

I am very appreciative of having the opportunity of sharing this simple message with you.

Do not follow the trend of society. You are children of God! It is so very important to hold on to the moral values we find in Christianity.

God and His works are evident in life and He works through us if we allow Him to.

The Lord always hears our prayers! He has blessed me tremendously by hearing mine, especially by blessing my baseball career.

On December 8, 1978, I accepted the Lord Jesus as my personal Savior. I will never forget that day which began my tremendous peace of mind and soul. Jesus has brought my life totally together.

I enjoy the Holy Bible. I especially appreciate the book of Proverbs in the Old Testament because it has so much wisdom for everyday living.

The Bible also helps me to overcome the fear

of death, because I know that Jesus has total control of my life!

Finally, there is a sticker on my van, and I would like you to strongly consider its message. It says, "Christians aren't perfect—they're just forgiven!"

It's promised in His Word,

Rudy May

Rudy May

Pitching experience, par excellence! Rudy May personifies experience and talent in the game of baseball. He has played on many different teams in both the American and National Leagues. During his baseball years he has pitched in thousands of major league innings, struck out over 1500 batters, and traveled continuously to baseball stadiums across the country.

Yet, Rudy's experience in life goes much deeper than the external glamour of the baseball world. He has found deep joy in his family life and in his life with God. He is a man who is deeply aware of the Lord in his life, and it is this awareness which brings him his deepest joy.

Rudy May is a warm, sincere, and grateful person. His message is down to earth but so very important. Carefully consider Rudy's message. Ponder over his message and draw from his pow-

erful witness inspiration and hope for yourselves.

Rudy May was a key factor in the 1980 divisional championship for the Yankees. He finished number one in the American League with a 2.46 ERA. He won fifteen games for the Yanks while losing only five. This .750 average was third best in the league.

Rudy proves his love for youth in many different ways. While he was a Baltimore Oriole he was a special friend to children at Johns Hopkins Hospital in Baltimore. He continuously makes appearances to young people at schools, clubs, and camps.

Recently, Rudy performed a generous act of service which I found very noble. He was scheduled to share some Christian relections with the children at Camp Don Bosco in Newton, New Jersey, on July 23, 1980, at 9:00 A.M. Because of rain delays, he was still pitching at Yankee Stadium after midnight during the previous evening. Although he had very little rest, Rudy still came to speak with the campers as he had promised. Considering the game, the travel to his home from the stadium, and the trip from his home in Teaneck, New Jersey, to northwestern New Jersey, Rudy had very little time to rest. I was inspired to tell him that the Lord would bless him for his generosity and sacrifice. He certainly was blessed, as he went on to play a truly outstanding season of major league baseball. Yet, more important than the victories in his pitching was his sense of peace even when he lost ball games.

Bobby Murcer

Dear Fans,

Take care of your total well-being and begin to do so early in life. It is so important to build a solid foundation for yourself when you are young so you may build upon it throughout your entire life.

I especially wish to share this important message with you: avoid drugs of any kind. You don't need to get high to be a good person. Unfortunately, getting high is often associated with being sociable. Be smart and be straight! Keep a firm hold over your own life at all times and learn not to follow negative influences.

It is so important for you to be a leader over your own self! Otherwise, there is no way that you will ever be able to lead others.

Bobby Murcer

Bobby Murcer

On August 6, 1979, Bobby Murcer played a game of baseball that rocked the universe! After delivering an emotional eulogy at the funeral of his friend and former Yankee teammate Thurman Munson, Bobby brought joy to a baseball world full of sorrow. In a nationally televised game, Bobby drove in all five Yankee runs to beat the 1979 American League champion Baltimore Orioles 5-4. Having been personally present at that explosive performance, I know I experienced a moment of sports history that will never be forgotten. Bobby's home run, the winning blast in the bottom of the ninth inning, joyfully electrified the entire stadium and, without a doubt, the entire baseball world.

Boby Murcer's message is one of extreme importance. Building a solid foundation while young is vital to building a personal life which will not fall easily when bombarded by false values such as drugs.

One cannot help but appreciate Bobby's patience in giving autographs to youth. One of my fellow religious brothers recently told me that he had once watched Bobby Murcer give out autographs to young people at Yankee Stadium for forty-five consecutive minutes before a game. On that day, Bobby Murcer added many more young people to his list of baseball fans, including an impressed religious brother.

Johnny Oates

Dear Fans,

First of all, I am presupposing that each of you has a basic belief in God, for before anything else in life, this is a necessity.

I wish to share some practical points with you. Besides believing in God, you must also believe in yourself and the gifts He has given to you. You must have faith in your own abilities to achieve even during times of difficulties. Try to eliminate any negative thoughts you may have about yourself and others so that your attitude may be positive and mature.

Also, you must learn how to express your feelings rather than holding grudges or negative attitude toward individuals. In the early years of my marriage, my wife and I had a communication problem. But with time, we both learned how to express our feelings in a proper manner, and since then our marriage has blossomed. We realized the importance of sharing, for whenever two or more people gather together differences of opinion are bound to occur. Therefore, it is very important for individuals to learn how to prudently express themselves whenever difficulties arise. This openness and sharing will bring tremendous growth to the parties involved.

Remember, be open and honest enough to share your thoughts rather than holding them only to yourselves. This very simple psychology will be a very positive factor in helping you to be a balanced person who realizes that proper communication is a necessity.

Johnny Oates

Johnny Oates

Johnny has now played major league baseball for one decade. During these years he has played for the Baltimore Orioles, Atlanta Braves, Philadelphia Phillies, Los Angeles Dodgers, and the New York Yankees.

Johnny received a Bachelor of Science Degree in Health and Physical Education from Virginia Tech (Virginia Polytechnic Institute and State University), where he played college ball before major league ball. He enjoys using his college education along with his baseball experience in teaching physical education to high school students during the major league's off-season.

Johnny Oates scores winning run in 13th inning—September 19, 1980. (*N.Y. Daily News* photo.)

Besides this youth work, Johnny has given many talks to Boy Scouts and various other youth groups. He has also enjoyed teaching the message of Christ as a Baptist Sunday school teacher.

Johnny is deeply aware of the pedestal on which many young people place him because of his major league status. Therefore, he always strives to be a good Christian example. He is very uncomfortable when some fans unfortunately shout out unnecessary comments to any athlete, since he feels this gives a bad example to the youths who are always present at any baseball stadium. Thanks to his own good example, Johnny successfully helps to combat some of this bad example.

Lou Piniella

Dear Fans,

There are a few thoughts I would like to impress upon you which might make you better athletes, but most importantly, I hope they will help to make you better human beings.

First, always remember that your mom and dad love you. When they give you advice, take it, and be sure to always listen to them. They were young once also and made some mistakes that have given them experience. They love you and want you to be the best person you can possibly be. Life in general becomes tougher as you grow older, so good advice received and practiced as a youngster will make it easier to be a well-rounded person later on.

Regarding athletics, take advice from your coaches, practice diligently, and work—especially on your weak points. Always have confidence in your ability and take pride in doing a good job. Remember to be a good sport. Place your emphasis not necessarily on winning or losing but on doing the best you can while enjoying fellowship with your peers. Don't let your success be determined by wins or losses.

Always remember that your education is going to be very important to you. The number of great amateur athletes that don't make it to the big leagues are many, so your education is of paramount importance.

Good luck to all of you! Practice being a good person early in life and it will be much easier for you to be good later on in life. Stay away from drugs; they will only hurt you. Pay strict attention to your teachers; they will definitely steer you in the right direction.

Best Always,
Lou Piniella

Lou Piniella

At the conclusion of Lou Piniella's baseball career, one will truly be able to say, "Admirable!" Lou has hit .300 or higher in five big league seasons. In close to fifteen years of major league experience, Lou had a .290 batting average as of 1980. Yankee fans will always be remembered as shouting "L-O-U" as he continuously delivered classy offensive and defensive clutch plays. Lou also has a fine pennant and World Series average which totals .286.

Lou Piniella's message is very important, and it is complementary to Bobby Murcer's. Bobby Murcer wrote about building a solid foundation while one is young. Lou Piniella writes that young adults should carry out the good advice they receive so that as they grow older they may profit from their efforts.

Throughout his professional baseball career, Lou Piniella has enjoyed sharing a positive message to youth at various banquets, clinics, hospitals, and schools.

Willie Randolph

Dear Fans,

Someone doesn't just become a superstar. It is a God-given gift—a gift which demands our total cooperation so that it may be perfected by discipline, dedication and hard work.

I am not a super human being. My gift from God is a very special one, but I want to love and be loved as a human being and not as some super-human who is out of touch with reality.

When I was young I received strength from Sunday services and the Word of God. This attitude was inspired by my family, which has always been deeply religious. I continue to praise the Lord Jesus for everything! I realize that without Him, I could do nothing!

Many people have tremendous talents. Yet, everyone should realize that whatever talents he has are gifts from God. Those who have been blessed must be humble and grateful for the gifts God has given them.

What a thrilling career God has given me! I have been in three World Series and selected for three All-Star games. But the Lord deserves the praise. I want everyone to know that I am glorifying His name by giving 100 percent effort all of the time. Whatever the results are I know the Lord is watching over me!

Finally, remember that the Lord's ways are not our ways. Because of an injury, I could not play in the 1978 World Series. My teammate, Brian Doyle, a beautiful Christian, took my place. God blessed Brian in that classic and allowed him to play tremendous ball. Yes, the Lord saw fit that it was Brian's time. The joy that this brought to Brian's life was matched by the joy I had for him. In God alone must we place all of our trust, for in His will is our joy.

Willie Randolph

Willie Randolph

Willie Randolph

Willie Randolph's offensive and defensive baseball abilities are outstanding. At a young age of twenty-seven, Willie had already appeared in five championship series, three World Series, and has been selected for three All-Star games.

Willie has an uncanny ability to reach base, and he ranks superbly in sacrifices, steals, hit-and-run plays, and constant clutch base hits.

At the same time, he is impressively humble! Willie realizes exactly where his sacrificially

Willie Randolph completing a double play. (*N.Y. Daily News* photo.)

developed gifts have come from. His humility impels him to want to be loved as a normal man, not as a superstar. Willie Randolph is a man who praises his Lord with his efforts and prays that others may give praise with their efforts to whom it is due.

Willie had another outstanding baseball season in 1980. He is also an outstanding person when he is off the baseball diamond. Willie often makes guest appearances to help youth. He especially likes to go to the Pilgrim Baptist Church in Brooklyn, New York, to share fellowship with the young people who worship there. Willie has worshiped the Lord in this Brooklyn church for many years; it is located in the same area where he grew up.

Willie has a good friend in baseball who plays for the Pittsburgh Pirates; his name is Willie Stargell, and he has his own foundation. Willie Stargell receives a lot of generous energy from Willie Randolph in his foundation that benefits sickle-cell anemia victims.

Willie Randolph also enjoys spreading his enthusiastic love of God by participating in the Fellowship of Christian Athletes.

Rudy May tells boys about the importance of Christ in his life at Camp Don Bosco in Newton, New Jersey—July 23, 1980. (Photo courtesy of Brother David Fletcher, SDB.)

Thurman Munson speaks to youth. (Photo by Edward Fitzgerald—courtesy of the Thornton-Donovan School.)

Brother Vince Bove with Bucky Dent at the Superdome in New Orleans, Louisiana—March 16, 1980. (Photo courtesy of Mike Dufrene.)

Brother Vince Bove with Reggie Jackson at the Superdome in New Orleans, Louisiana—March 16, 1980. (Photo courtesy of Mike Dufrene.)

Brian Doyle, Brother Vince Bove and Rick Cerone at Yankee Stadium—October 3, 1980. (Photo courtesy of Anthony Damiani.)

Brother Vince Bove showing Yankee testimonials to Cardinal Cooke at Yankee Stadium—September 5, 1980. (Photo by Chris Sheridan.)

Former Yankee slugger and Hall-of-Famer Mickey Mantle.

Yankees' "Greatest Player Ever" at First Base—Lou Gehrig.

Yankees' "Greatest Player Ever" in Right Field—Babe Ruth.

Yankees' "Greatest Player Ever" in Center Field—Joe Di Maggio.

"The Ole Perfesser"—Casey Stengel.

At bat, Yankee great Roger Maris.

Famous former Yankee and Hall-of-Famer Whitey Ford.

George Herman "Babe" Ruth slams another home run. (*N.Y. Daily News* photo.)

A mighty swing by Hall-of-Famer Joe Di Maggio. (*N.Y. Daily News* photo.)

Lou Gehrig signs his 1937 contract for $36,700 while Jacob Ruppert, Joe McCarthy and Joe Di Maggio look on. (*N.Y. Daily News* photo.)

Our beloved friend, Thurman Munson. (N.Y. *Daily News* photo.)

Old Timers Day at Yankee Stadium (June 21, 1980). From left to right: DiMaggio, Mantle, Maris, Martin, Berra and Ford. (Photo by Louis Requena.)

Bobby Richardson

Dear Fans,

My background has been primarily athletics, first as a player in the Little League programs of South Carolina, then on the high school level, and then the wonderful opportunity of signing and playing with the New York Yankees during a time when they were constantly in World Series play.

In my first years there were some very difficult times, and in particular, I remember a letter from my high school coach that reminded me of a decision I had made to receive Jesus Christ as Lord and Savior. During these difficult times, I understood the meaning of the verse in Matthew 6:33 that says: "But seek ye first the kingdom of God, and his righteousness; and all these things shall be added unto you." If I were to in any way try to sum up my own life or to inspire other young people, I would just say simply it's so very important to know and love and walk daily with the Lord Jesus Christ; and in the realm of athletics, I think the American athlete can be a great exponent of the Christian witness in our land today, and I am excited to see athletes taking a stand for the person of Christ in their lives.

Sincerely,
Bobby Richardson

Bobby Richardson

Bobby Richardson played for more than a decade with the New York Yankees and remains appreciated as one of baseball's all-time best second basemen.

Defensively, Bobby was noted for his quickness, strong arm, and great catching range. These defensive talents helped Bobby to win the prestigious Golden Glove Award as best second baseman from 1961-65. Offensively, Bobby had two years with a batting average over .300, along with his exceptional World Series exploits with the bat. In the 1960 World Series against the Pittsburgh Pirates, Bobby exploded with twelve runs batted in on eleven hits, including a grand-slam home run, two doubles, and two triples.

As a Yankee, Bobby was appreciated by his teammates for his outstanding and sincere Christian example. He had a presence which

inspired respect for his Christian beliefs. This respect for Bobby still remains in the memories of many of his former teammates and baseball associates.

Bobby remains a dedicated Christian who deeply appreciates the blessings the Lord has given to him and his loved ones. He is aware of where his gifts originate and who he must serve. He is a devoted church and civic leader. He is also active in the Fellowship of Christian Athletes.

Besides his many public speaking engagements, Bobby has shared his love for Christ in a book entitled *Grand Slam.* This book incorporates the principles of baseball with the Christian life.

Phil Rizzuto

Dear Fans,

Prior to the last few years, there had been a decline in the faith people should have in God. Fortunately it seems we have made positive progress toward a new upsurge in the faith we so desperately need—faith in God.

I am proud of my Catholic tradition. Yet, I appreciate the values so many religions offer. It is great to see people worshiping God especially when families do so together.

Religion has always been a very important aspect of my life. My faith in God has given me the strength to pull through many trials. One trial which I particularly remember happened when I was seventeen years old and playing for the Yankee farm team, which was located, at that time, in Bassett, Virginia. While playing, I stepped in a deep hole (we used to call these hard-to-see pitfalls "gopher holes"). I severed a leg muscle, which thereafter led to a serious infection and gangrene. An operation was a necessity.

I remember fervently praying the rosary in Our Lady's honor before the initial time of operation. When I awoke in the recovery room I found the rosaries in my hand, so I continued to pray. I was scared because the doctor had told me I would never play baseball again, but I put all my trust in God. During the period of my recuperation I made continuous novenas and Holy Communions. Without a doubt, God pulled me through and set me on a path of a very blessed baseball career.

Trials have often touched my life, but the Lord has always been there to give me strength. May all of you realize the importance of worshiping Him, for He desires to be your source of strength and blessings also.

Phil Rizzuto

Phil Rizzuto

Phil Rizzuto is considered by many baseball fans to have been the greatest shortstop in Yankee history. He played with the Yanks for fifteen years, from 1941 through 1956. These were some of the greatest years in Yankee baseball history, as is evident in Phil's participation in a spectacular number of World Series—

nine in all.

Since the completion of his playing days in 1956, "Scooter" Rizzuto has become the greatest broadcaster in Yankee history. He has provided Yankee fans with unmatched enthusiasm for the Yanks during his twenty-four years behind the microphone.

His enthusiasm for the Yanks is on a par with his enthusiastic concern for young people. One evening, Phil made a profound statement as he and I sat in his broadcasting booth watching the multitude enter Yankee Stadium: "I have no doubt in my mind that youths need and really want God in their lives more than anything else."

One cannot help but appreciate Phil's love and concern for the fans, as he can often be heard wishing them birthday, anniversary, congratulations, and get-well greetings on the air. The fans' love for him is mutual. I was at the stadium on September 25, 1980, when the greatest thrill in the park that evening was to hear all the fans in Yankee Stadium sing "Happy Birthday" to the Yankee Rizzuto whom they love so much.

Phil has received many awards for his service to young people throughout his career. Yet, his favorite award remains the one which he first received as a Yankee from his young fans in 1941. The award was presented to him by the Catholic Youth Organization for being their "most popular Yankee." Interestingly, Phil was presented with this prized possession by His

Eminence Terence Cardinal Cooke, whom Phil recalls at that time was Father Terence Cooke.

It is obvious to anyone who ever heard of Yankee baseball that Phil Rizzuto loves the fans, young and old, and that the fans love Phil Rizzuto.

Aurelio Rodriguez

Dear Fans,

I grew up in a strict Catholic atmosphere, which helped me to realize firmly the importance of God. I believe this background was a very positive foundation for my life as a Christian.

As I think about my own days as a young man, I realize that life in Mexico was harsh. Today, it seems that life is so much different. As young people, you have a very different life style in comparison to my life as a youth. Yet, one thing remains changeless, man must always realize that he needs God.

All of us must turn to God often, not only when we need help, but we must also be able to thank Him during good times as well. We must also respect His holy Word. When we treat this Word with reverence, it can cause tremendous results.

Recently, I knew of a person who was constantly in trouble. Then, he began to appreciate the Bible. Since then, he has totally accepted Christ and has changed his life in such a positive way. He now is a good Christian, and he constantly helps children in a poor orphanage in Mexico.

Let us always be willing to hear God as He speaks to us through the Holy Bible. For His Word can help us to live a better life, a life full of His blessings.

Aurelio Rodriguez

Aurelio Rodriguez

Aurelio Rodriguez

Aurelio Rodriguez played for the Detroit Tigers for nine consecutive years before he became a New York Yankee in 1980. He had a fine defensive playing reputation during these years, which he has maintained as a Yankee. Interestingly enough, Aurelio led the Yanks in sacrifice bunts even though he missed the first four months of the Yankee season.

During the off-season, Aurelio is a special friend to the children of the Catholic orphanage in his home town of Los Mochis, Mexico. Besides his casual visits to these children, he always makes sure that many of them are his guests at the nearby stadium where he plays baseball during the major league off-season.

(Photo by Louis Requena.)

Pete Sheehy

Dear Fans,

Ever since my very early years as a boy I can remember attending catechism classes during the week. In these classes I learned about God, and I expressed my love for Him by never missing Sunday Mass.

Even though I am now over seventy years old, I still realize the importance of going to Sunday Mass. I love my home parish of Our Lady of Victories in Huntington, New Jersey. I especially enjoy the warm fellowship the parishioners share with each other before and after each Mass. Yet, even when I am on a road trip with the Yankees, I always make sure I am faithful to my obligation of attending Sunday Mass.

During my years of military service in World War II, I can remember appreciating the importance of Mass. As an army soldier between the years of 1942 and 1945, I was stationed in Guam and Okinawa. My outfit had a very wonderful priest as chaplain; the men loved him very much. He helped me tremendously as I struggled in those difficult times by making me realize that God and His Mother were with me and that they would help me. I remember his words in a special way on one particular occasion when I was on the front line of battle. I was pinned down because of the continuous gunfire and artillery. I was saying continuous Hail Marys and promising God that if He allowed me to survive, I would never again complain. I had close calls during those days, but I believe that the Mother of God helped me. I have been faithful to my promise of never again complaining ever since.

I hope that in some small way my own story can encourage you to fulfill your own Christian obligations of attending Sunday services and that you will also avoid unnecessary complaining in every possible way.

Pete Sheehy

Pete Sheehy (Yankee Clubhouse Manager)

Little did Pete Sheehy realize that his assistance to the Yankee locker room manager for free tickets in 1927 would lead him to a fifty-three-year stint with the Yankees.

Pete has humbly tended to all the menial tasks

in the players' clubhouse since that first day in 1927. He has earned a very respected reputation among the players as being a man who is dedicated, trustworthy, and silent. Due to his quiet disposition, his first clubhouse manager nicknamed him "Silent Pete" on Pete's first day in the clubhouse in 1927. The name has remained with this official, honorary Yankee, whose real name is Michael Joseph Sheehy.

Because of his many years of appreciated service, there hangs a plaque on the clubhouse entrance which reads: "The Pete Sheehy Clubhouse." It was named in his honor when the new Yankee Stadium reopened in 1976.

Pete believes that his main responsibility toward helping young people involves the players he serves in the Yankee clubhouse. He is now in his seventies. The difference in age between him and the players has made Pete sort of a father and grandfather figure to many different players for many years. Pete is sincerely dedicated to serving them and especially those whom "Silent Pete" says "are the bottom men on the totem pole. These are the men I really try to serve in a very special way."

Eric Soderholm

Dear Fans,

Four years ago, I can remember lying in a hospital bed and peeking under my heavily bandaged left knee. There I saw two scars, each about eight inches long. Then, when the doctor came in and told me that my chances of ever playing baseball again were slim because the operation was extremely tough, well, I broke down and cried like a baby. But, you know, I'll always be thankful for the doctor telling me that, because it created a burning desire inside me to prove him wrong.

I went into a heavy weight-training program by Nautilus for eight months. I missed the entire season in 1976, but through a lot of hard work, I came back in 1977 and signed with the Chicago White Six, where I went on to hit .280 with twenty-five home runs. I was awarded the American League "Comeback Player of the Year." I guess I did prove him wrong, but the real message here is the old saying: "If you think you can, you are right. If you think you can't, you're right again."

There will always be obstacles in your road to happiness and success, but strong is the person who learns to overcome. One of my favorite sayings is "God doesn't make junk." With that in mind, go out and be the best you can be at whatever you choose to be.

Your Friend,

Eric Soderholm
Yankees

Eric Soderholm

Eric Soderholm's inspirational comeback story can soften the hardest of hearts. After five years of defensive and offensive baseball in the Minnesota Twins organization, tragedy seemed to devastate Eric's career. In 1976, Eric partially tore the cartilage in his left knee. After having this knee operated on, Eric was told that his career in baseball was over. Eric also had broken some of his ribs in a construction accident.

Eric's courageous perseverance inspired him to engage in vigorous athletic conditioning and extensive weight training. By unanimous decision, Eric was awarded the 1977 American League Comeback Player of the Year Award

after an incredible season with the Chicago White Sox.

Eric's physical obstacles have been overcome by his sheer determination to scale any mountains of difficulty that try to block his path.

Eric has given many talks to people of all ages throughout his major leage baseball career. He is a very warm and sensitive person who remembers breaking down and crying during two separate speaking engagements. The first time was when he received his American League Comeback Player of the Year Award in 1977. The second time when Eric publicly broke down and cried was during a testimonial before a group of his sister's business associates. While Eric was speaking about the difficulties his physical trials brought to him in 1976, he noticed that his sister was crying as she listened. Being touched by his sister's emotions, Eric also began to cry during his presentation. This caused a chain reaction among the members of the audience, and many others began to shed tears. Eric realizes that his witness expressed through tears on that day gave greater testimony than anything he could have said.

Luis Tiant

Dear Fans,

The greatest message I have to share with you is to believe in God and have faith in His words. Whether you are experiencing good times or bad, remember that life has its share of both, but God always has everything in control.

Sometimes God allows us to go through periods of difficulty, but if we have faith, we will become better individuals through trials. God is there, and when we work to help ourselves, He will bless us.

In my own baseball career, I have had many ups and downs. Especially during my last twelve years, I have had many trials. Often people thought I was finished as a ballplayer and that I should give up pitching. But with God's help I have always pulled through.

Remember that God must always be first in your life. Don't turn to Him only when you think you need Him, because you always do need Him. Turn to Him often, trying to have the right intention rather than allowing it to become routine.

Remember also to try and get along with everyone, but never give up God because of what some friends of yours might think.

Finally, I ask you to develop a positive attitude toward life, appreciating all the good things God gives you. Don't be a negative person who complains about little problems. Compared to others, you may be very lucky. It would be sad to complain about a little cut while someone is suffering with a terrible disease. Remember, God is always present and He loves each of us so very much.

Luis Tiant

Luis Tiant

As of 1980, Luis Tiant was forty years old and still playing successful major league baseball. He is certainly a prized and appreciated veteran of the game.

Luis's major league career began in 1964 when he pitched for the Cleveland Indians, whom he played with for six consecutive seasons. Afterwards, Luis played for one year with the Minnesota Twins and then for the Boston Red

Sox, from 1971 through 1978. As a Red Sox pitcher, Luis played on two All-Star teams and won two games in the 1975 World Series.

Along with his Yankee teammates, Luis has a great appreciation for young people, which he has expressed by often visiting children who are sick.

Prior to the 1981 baseball season, Luis Tiant became a free agent. Soon after, he signed with the Pittsburgh Pirates organization.

Tommy Underwood

Dear Fans,

When I was a young man, I was impressed by a banner in my parish church which read, "What you are is God's gift to you, what you make of yourself is your gift to God."

This slogan has been an inspiration to me for the past fifteen years. I am very aware of the gifts God has given to me, especially for the good influence He has given me through my parents. I also realize that my ability to play major league baseball comes as a gift from God.

The mere fact that we exist is a reason to be grateful to God. Also, each of you has your own particular gifts. Remember that whatever gifts you have received must be worked on and developed. Strive to make yourselves the best persons that God has meant each of you to be.

Your efforts and the results which follow will be your gift back to God.

Tommy Underwood (signature)

Tommy Underwood

Tommy Underwood

Although Tommy Underwood is only twenty-seven years old, he already has six and one-half years of major league pitching experience. He helped the 1980 Yankees clinch their fourth American League East title in five years with his fine pitching. His starting and bullpen pitching led him to a career high of thirteen wins in 1980.

Tommy's own particular service toward young people takes place when he visits his alma mater of St. Joan of Arc School in Indiana to speak with youths each year. He has also enjoyed being of service to the St. Jude Children's Research Hospital in Tennessee. This hospital cares for children who are afflicted with the most debilitating kinds of childhood diseases. Tommy has served the children of this hospital in many ways, including being honorary chairman of a St. Jude radiothon in his home town of Kokomo, Indiana.

Bob Watson

Dear Fans,

Have no fear in setting a difficult goal for yourselves and striving to meet it. And in striving to achieve reaching your goal, I would like you to consider these two key points: sacrifice and discipline.

Sacrifice and discipline are important aspects of everyday living. The secret of applying them is drawn from our Christian life. We learn exactly what sacrifice and discipline are in Christianity.

Learning to accept the bitter and the sweet are integral aspects of living a life of sacrifice and discipline, so learn to accept each when they come your way.

We learn from Christianity that to receive we must learn how to give. Be generous in regard to your sacrifices and disciplines. The more generous you are, the more blessed you will be.

Bob Watson

Bob Watson

Bob Watson

Bob Watson's major league totals are certainly remarkable. Besides being the man who providentially scored the millionth run in baseball, Bob has had over fifteen years of major league experience. His statistics for these years speak boldly. Bob has had over 1600 big league hits with a .319 American League batting average and a .297 National League batting average. These give him a combined total average of .300.

The giant, 212-pound, six-foot-two first baseman and valuable designated hitter is most certainly an asset to the winning Yankee heritage.

Bob Watson's values are very noble ones. As the New York Yankee Team chaplain, he also strives to instill these values within his teammates by his words—and, most importantly, by his example.

Bob has served his Lord in many ways besides being the Yankee team chaplain, who is responsible for coordinating prayer services for his teammates. During his nine years with the Houston Astros, between 1970 and 1979, Bob

gave frequent talks to various youth groups. He also helped the young people of Houston through the Big Brother program. He and his wife, Carol, found great joy in serving their congregation at St. Stephen's Episcopal Church in Houston by offering their time and efforts to the church's various needs.

Dennis Werth

Dear Fans,

An important attitude to have regarding any career one chooses is dedication. This dedication must have its roots in the little things one does each day.

From as early as I can remember I have always had a positive and constructive dedication to my responsibilities. No matter what my responsibilities were, I always put my heart into fulfilling them well. There is a tremendous value in doing small things well. So whether you are playing baseball, doing homework, or dumping the garbage, do it well!

I appreciate being a big league ballplayer, but I know that true dedication can bring happiness to anyone in any career. Be dedicated to whatever you are doing. Put your whole heart into doing all things well, and enjoy the satisfaction and joy that will follow.

Dennis Werth

Dennis Werth

Dennis Werth

Dennis Werth is a Yankee who is full of major league character. While Dennis was on the Yankee AAA team he proved himself to be a ballplayer beyond any doubt. The six-one, 200-pound, versatile fielder has held high batting averages in the Yankee farm system. He certainly will be right at home in the big leagues.

Dennis's positive attitude and spirit of dedication will certainly motivate him to have an explosive career. Yet, Dennis knows very well that happiness strikes home with anyone who is dedicated to fulfilling his obligations with sincere efforts.

His realization of his responsibility toward young people has often led Dennis to share instructional techniques at various youth clinics and camps.

On August 24, 1980, Dennis renewed his special commitment to Christ by being baptized. He plans to live out this personal commitment by serving the Lord to the best of his abilities. This service will often lead him to help youths.

(Photo by Louis Requena.)

Final Reflections

Dear Fans,

Serve the Lord with joy! This short yet profound expression beautifully sums up how I feel about my work in preparing *And on the Eighth Day God Created the Yankees*. I have learned so very deeply that it has been the Lord's providence that has ordained this book to come into existence. He has desired it, and I am blessed to be the one He has chosen to be His instrument in this service—a service that has been full of joy!

The Lord's inspiration for this book unveiled itself to me very gradually. Let me share with you how it developed.

In August, 1979, Yankee catcher and captain Thurman Munson lost his life in a tragic plane crash. Many felt a deep sense of personal loss, yet through this sorrow God was to bring about so much good.

Shortly after Thurman's death, I was enjoying the pregame warm-ups of the players at Yankee

Stadium. It was here that God's work with them through me began. As I watched, I sensed an emptiness within the practicing players, who had been deeply affected by the death of their teammate Thurman. I prayed for these players. Then I put my prayers into action. I asked a security guard to get Bucky Dent's attention for me. Upon seeing me as a man of the cloth, Bucky Dent came over to me without hesitation. We spoke but for a few moments, but these were grace-filled moments of Christian fellowship. Bucky then invited me to be his guest at the next evening's game, and I quickly accepted. Bucky and I continued to become friends and before long he was introducing me to his fellow Yankees in their clubhouse. Many of the players and I established a fine rapport and remained friendly throughout the season.

Becoming more and more associated with these players gave me a wonderful opportunity to share Christ's gospel message with them. Christ also inspired me to encourage them to share His message with those who admired them.

The impact that even one individual can have on the lives of others can be awesome! One need only reflect on the humble life of Jesus of Nazareth, who has been the central focus of the human race for over nineteen centuries.

In my own life I have been so deeply inspired by Christ and by a great man who reflected this Nazarene's image, especially for youth, that is, St. John Bosco. Without his Christlike inspiration, I would never be a religious nor would this book exist.

John Bosco was born of a poor family in northern Italy in 1815. He spent his early years working on a farm while struggling to find time in between busy farm chores for his schooling. From his earliest years he overcame constant difficulties to achieve his goal, the Catholic priesthood.

As a young priest, John Bosco began to gather boys together. He built playgrounds, workshops, and classrooms for them. His work expanded as boys were continually drawn to him by his fatherly concern and love. Some of these boys also became priests and helped him to form his own religious society. This society, now known as the Salesians of St. John Bosco, would use reason, religion, and kindness to touch the lives of youth everywhere. Now, there are over 35,000 Salesian priests, brothers, and sisters of St. John Bosco, who work for millions of youth in over ninety countries throughout the entire world. I am deeply grateful to God for allowing me to be one of these many sons and daughters of St. John Bosco.

As a Salesian of St. John Bosco, dedicated to the Christian Education of youth, it is my most intense desire that this book touch the hearts of fans everywhere, especially the hearts of the young. I believe that young and old everywhere are starving for God. May this book help to satisfy some of that hunger, a hunger that can only be satisfied by Christ. St. John Bosco's work continues, even if but one of the players in this book inspires one person, young or young-at-heart, to love Christ more.

I am deeply grateful to those who have allowed God to use them in making this book possible, especially the Yankee players. It is my fervent prayer that Christ will give them the courage needed to live the faith they have expressed through this book. I also wish to thank the Yankee management, Diana Munson, and the credited photographers. I am especially grateful to my fellow Salesians for their encouragement and prayerful support. Most importantly, I am humbly grateful to God for His continuous blessings upon me and this publication.

I pray that you may obtain some positive inspiration from this book. Also, I am available for any appropriate service I can render, from offering information on St. John Bosco and the Salesians to sharing Christian encouragement and hope with you. I am also available for guest appearances to share more with the public, both information about the book and the joy of living the gospel message. I would be happy to hear from you and serve you.

May the Lord continue to send His Spirit to touch the hearts of His people everywhere!

Sincerely in Christ,

Brother Vince Bove S.D.B.

Brother Vince Bove, S.D.B.
Box T, 148 Main Street
New Rochelle, New York 10802

Brother Vince Bove with Brian Doyle at Yankee Stadium. (Photo by Anthony Damiani.)

About the Author

Since his boyhood on the streets of the Bronx in New York City, Brother Vince Bove has been involved with sports—baseball, stickball, track, soccer, wrestling and basketball.

His background has enabled him to pursue his vocation—helping young people who are attracted to sports. His present ministry as a Salesian of Don Bosco utilizes sports as a means of reaching youth with the message of the Gospel. He can be found coaching soccer, for example, and has led a team to a state championship. He also serves as a lifeguard and teaches swimming during summer camp. He competes in track and field events; to keep in shape, he runs thirty miles per week. He can be found working with young men on basketball courts, football and baseball fields, in weight rooms and other places of athletic participation.

Brother Vince, on his journey toward the

Salesian priesthood, received a B.A. in philosophy from Don Bosco College in Newton, New Jersey, in 1977. Upon graduation, he taught theology and coached soccer for two years at Archbishop Shaw High School in Marrero, Louisiana. He is presently teaching at Salesian High School in New Rochelle, New York. In the near future, he will begin his theological studies in direct preparation for his ordination as a priest.

Brother Vince's great desire to help young people led him to write *And on the Eighth Day God Created the Yankees*. It is a reflection of his vigorous ministry and his spiritual concern for today's youth.

Additional copies of *And on the Eighth Day God Created the Yankees* can be ordered through better bookstores.

If ordering by mail, send $4.95 plus $1.00 postage and handling to:

Logos/Haven Books
201 Church Street
Plainfield, NJ 07060

Include the book's title and your name and address.